Lights! Camera! Action!

Creative teams produce great performances.

SCHOLASTIC
LITERACY PLACE®

Copyright acknowledgments and credits appear on page 160, which constitutes an extension of this copyright page.

Copyright © 1996 by Scholastic Inc.   All rights reserved.   Printed in the U.S.A.
ISBN 0-590-49100-8

3 4 5 6 7 8 9 10   23   02 01 00 99 98 97 96

2

Have Fun at
a Children's Theater

**Creative teams
produce great
performances.**

Strike Up the Band

We come together to put on a performance.

Cast and Crew

Performances combine the talents of many people.

Showtime!

Clear plans and directions help team members create projects.

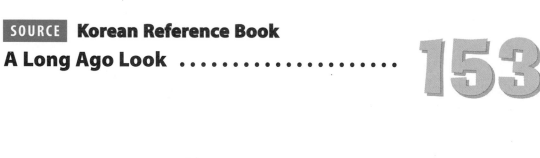

Trade Books

The following books accompany this *Lights! Camera! Action!* SourceBook.

Humorous Fiction
Baseball Ballerina
by Kathryn Cristaldi
illustrated by Abby Carter

Fantasy
Sheep Dreams
by Arthur A. Levine
illustrated by Judy Lanfredi

Realistic Fiction
Song and Dance Man Caldecott Award
by Karen Ackerman
illustrated by
Stephen Gammell

Big Book

Fantasy
The Bunny Play
by Loreen Leedy

8

Strike Up the Band

We come together to put on a performance.

Watch the unusual show four animals put on for some robbers.

Join in the music celebration in two different communities.

The Bremen Town
Musicians

by HANS WILHELM

AWARD
WINNING

Author/
Illustrator

There was once a donkey
whose master made him carry sacks
to the mill year after year.
Now the donkey was getting old,
and his strength began to fail.

When the master realized that the donkey
was of no use to him anymore,
he decided to get rid of him.
But the donkey guessed
that something bad was in the wind,
so he made up his mind to run away.

He thought he would take the road to Bremen,
where he might get an engagement as a town musician.

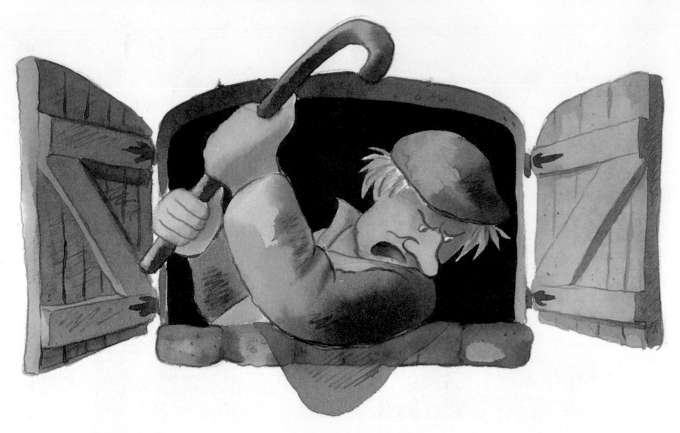

On the way,
he found a dog lying by the side of the road,
panting as if he had been running for a long time.
"Now, Holdfast, why are you so out of breath?"
asked the donkey.

"Oh, dear!" said the dog. "I am old and getting weaker
every day, and I can no longer hunt.
My master was going to kill me, but I escaped!
Now how am I to make a living?"

"I will tell you what," said the donkey.
"I am going to Bremen to become a town musician.
Come with me. I can play the lute,
and you can beat the drum."

The dog liked the idea, and they walked on together.

It was not long before they came to a cat sitting by
the roadside, looking as dismal as three wet days.
"Now then, what is the matter with you, old Whiskerwiper?"
asked the donkey.

"Who can be cheerful when his life is in danger?"
answered the cat. "Now that I am old, my teeth are getting blunt,
and I'd rather sit by the fire than chase after mice.
Because of this, my mistress wanted to drown me,
so I ran away. But now I don't know what is
to become of me."

"Come with us to Bremen," said the donkey,
"and be a town musician. You know how to serenade."

The cat liked the idea and went along with them.

Soon the three runaways passed by a yard.
A rooster was perched on top of the gate,
crowing as loudly as he could.
"Your cries are breaking my heart," said the donkey.
"What is the matter?"

"Tomorrow is Sunday and I have foretold good weather,"
said the rooster, "but my mistress is expecting guests
and has ordered the cook to cut off my head
and put me in the soup.
Therefore, I cry with all my might
while I still can."

"You'd better come along with us, Redhead," the donkey said.
"We are going to Bremen to become town musicians.
We could do with a powerful voice like yours."

This sounded perfect to the rooster, so all four went on together.

But Bremen was too far to be reached in one day.
Towards evening they came to a forest
where they decided to spend the night.

The donkey and the dog lay down under a huge tree,
the cat found a place among the branches,
and the rooster flew up to the top of the tree where he felt safe.
But before he went to sleep, the rooster looked all around
to the four points of the compass.
Suddenly he saw a small light shining in the distance.

He called out to his friends,
"There must be a house over there."

"Let's go and see," said the donkey,
"for this place is not very comfortable."

"And there might be
a few bones," said the dog.

They all set off in the direction of the light.
It grew larger and larger until it led them
to a robber's house, all lighted up.

The donkey—who was the tallest—
went to the window and looked in.
"Well, what do you see?" asked the dog.

"What do I see?" answered the donkey.
"I see a table loaded with wonderful
things to eat and to drink. And
robbers are sitting around the table,
having a great time!"

"That would be perfect for us!"
said the rooster.

"Yes, indeed," replied the donkey.
"I wish we were there."

The four friends put their heads together
to decide how they might scare off the robbers.
Finally they knew what to do.

The donkey placed his forefeet on the windowsill.
The dog got on the donkey's back,
the cat stood on the top of the dog, and lastly,
the rooster flew up and perched
on the cat's head.

At a given signal, they all
began to perform their music.
The donkey brayed,
the dog barked,
the cat meowed,
and the rooster crowed!

Then they burst into the room,
breaking the windowpanes.
The robbers fled at the dreadful noise.
They thought it was some goblin
and ran to the forest in the utmost terror.

27

The four friends sat down at the table
and feasted as if they hadn't eaten for weeks.
When they had finished they put out the lights
and looked for places to sleep.
The donkey found a comfortable spot outside,
the dog lay down behind the door,
the cat curled up on the hearth by the warm ashes,
and the rooster settled himself in the loft.
And since they were all very tired from their long journey,
they soon fell asleep.

In the forest, from a safe distance away,
the robbers were watching the house the whole time.
Shortly after midnight they saw that no light was burning
and that everything appeared peaceful.

"We shouldn't have been such cowards and run away!" said their leader, and he ordered one of them to go back and check out the house.

The robber went into the house and found everything very quiet.

He went into the kitchen to strike a light, and the cat woke up.
Thinking that the cat's glowing eyes were burning coals,
the robber held a match to them in order to light it.
The cat did not find this funny. He flew into the robber's
face, spitting and scratching.

The robber screamed in terror
and ran to get out through
the back door. But the dog,
who was lying there, leaped up
and bit the robber's leg.

The frightened robber rushed into
the yard where the donkey
struck out and gave him
a great kick with his hind foot.

And the rooster,
who had been wakened
by the noise, cried his loudest,
"Kee-ka-ree-kee!"

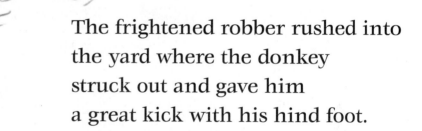

The robber ran back to the others
as fast as he could,
and said, "Oh, dear!
In that house there is a gruesome witch.
I felt her breath, and she scratched me
with her long nails.
And by the door there stands a monster
who stabbed me in the leg with a knife.
And in the yard there lies a fierce giant
who beat me with a club.
And on the roof
there sits a judge
who cried, 'Bring the thief to me!'
I got out of that place as fast as I could!"

This scared the robbers so much that they never
went back to that house again.

And the four musicians liked their new home
so much that they stayed forever
and never went to Bremen Town at all.

Our big chair often sits in our living room empty now.

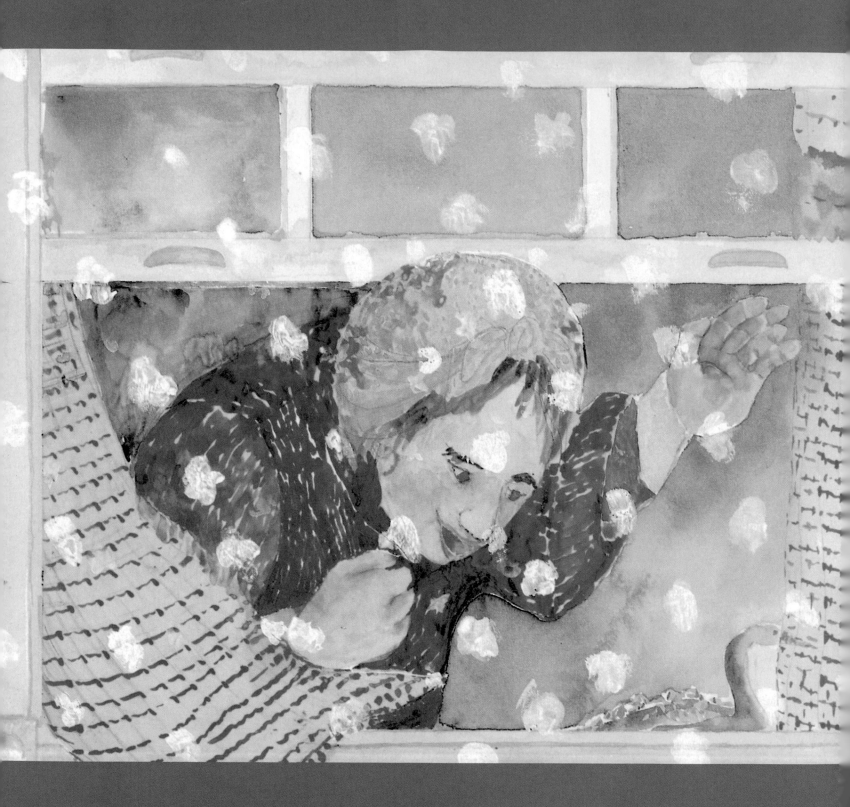

38

When I first got my accordion, Grandma and Mama used to sit in that chair together to listen to me practice. And every day after school while Mama was at her job at the diner, Grandma would be sitting in the chair by the window. Even if it was snowing big flakes down on her hair, she would lean way out to call, "Hurry up, Pussycat. I've got something nice for you."

But now Grandma is sick. She has to stay upstairs in the big bed in Aunt Ida and Uncle Sandy's extra room. Mama and Aunt Ida and Uncle Sandy and I take turns taking care of her. When I come home from school, I run right upstairs to ask Grandma if she wants anything. I carry up the soup Mama has left for her. I water her plants and report if the Christmas cactus has any flowers yet. Then I sit on her bed and tell her about everything.

Grandma likes it when my friends Leora, Jenny, and Mae come home with me because we play music for her. Leora plays the drums. Mae plays the flute. Jenny plays fiddle and I play my accordion. One time we played a dance for Grandma that we learned in the music club at school.

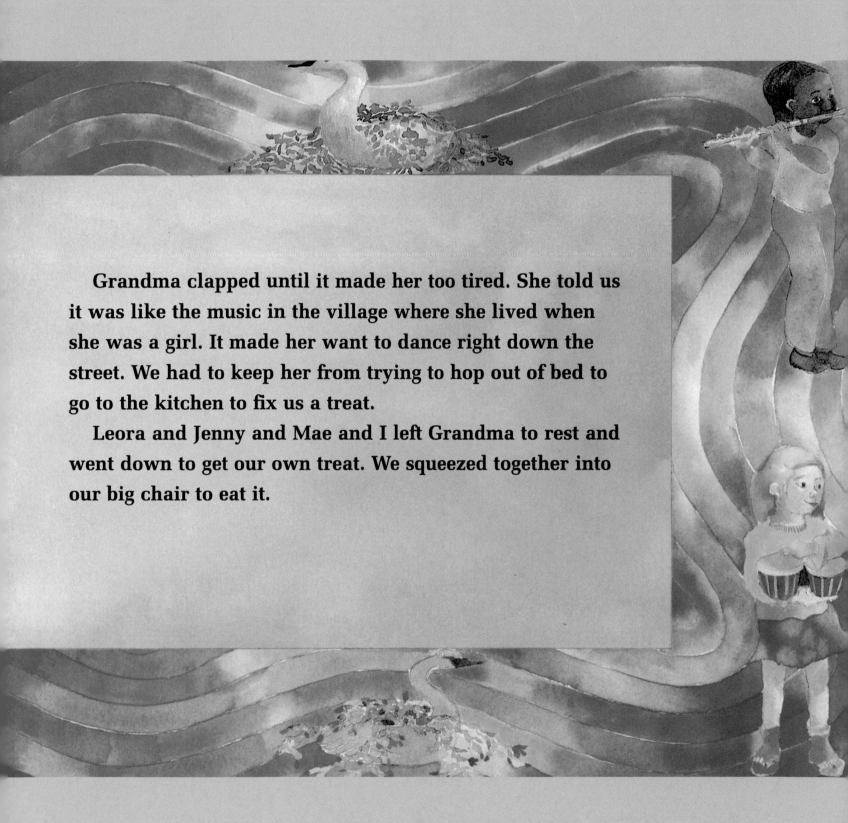

Grandma clapped until it made her too tired. She told us it was like the music in the village where she lived when she was a girl. It made her want to dance right down the street. We had to keep her from trying to hop out of bed to go to the kitchen to fix us a treat.

Leora and Jenny and Mae and I left Grandma to rest and went down to get our own treat. We squeezed together into our big chair to eat it.

"It feels sad down here without your grandma," Leora said. "Even your big money jar up there looks sad and empty."

"Remember how it was full to the top and I couldn't even lift it when we bought the chair for my mother?" I said.

"And remember how it was more than half full when you got your accordion?" Jenny said.

"I bet it's empty now because your mother has to spend all her money to take care of your grandma till she gets better. That's how it was when my father had his accident and couldn't go to work for a long time," Mae said.

Mae had a dime in her pocket and she dropped it into the jar. "That will make it look a little fuller anyway," she said as she went home.

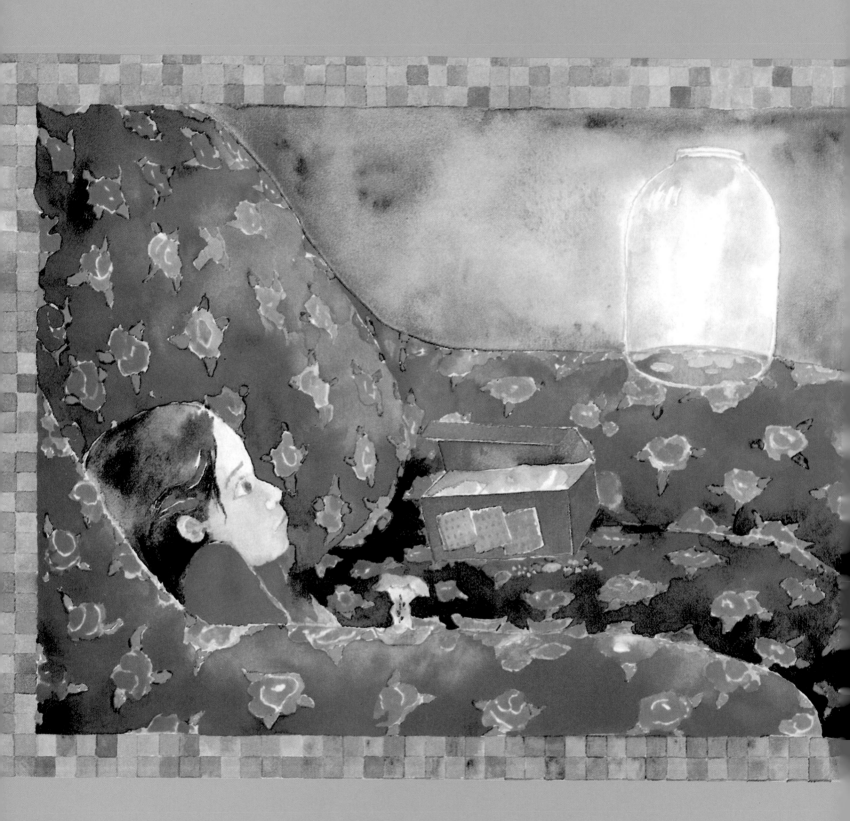

But after Jenny and Leora and Mae went home, our jar looked even emptier to me. I wondered how we would ever be able to fill it up again while Grandma was sick. I wondered when Grandma would be able to come downstairs again. Even our beautiful chair with roses all over it seemed empty with just me in the corner of it. The whole house seemed so empty and so quiet.

48

I got out my accordion and I started to play. The notes sounded beautiful in the empty room. One song that is an old tune sounded so pretty I played it over and over. I remembered what my mother had told me about my other grandma and how she used to play the accordion. Even when she was a girl not much bigger than I, she would get up and play at a party or a wedding so the company could dance and sing. Then people would stamp their feet and yell, "More, more!" When they went home, they would leave money on the table for her.

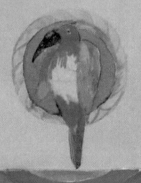

That's how I got my idea for how I could help fill up the jar again. I ran right upstairs. "Grandma," I whispered. "Grandma?"

"Is that you, Pussycat?" she answered in a sleepy voice. "I was just having such a nice dream about you. Then I woke up and heard you playing that beautiful old song. Come. Sit here and brush my hair."

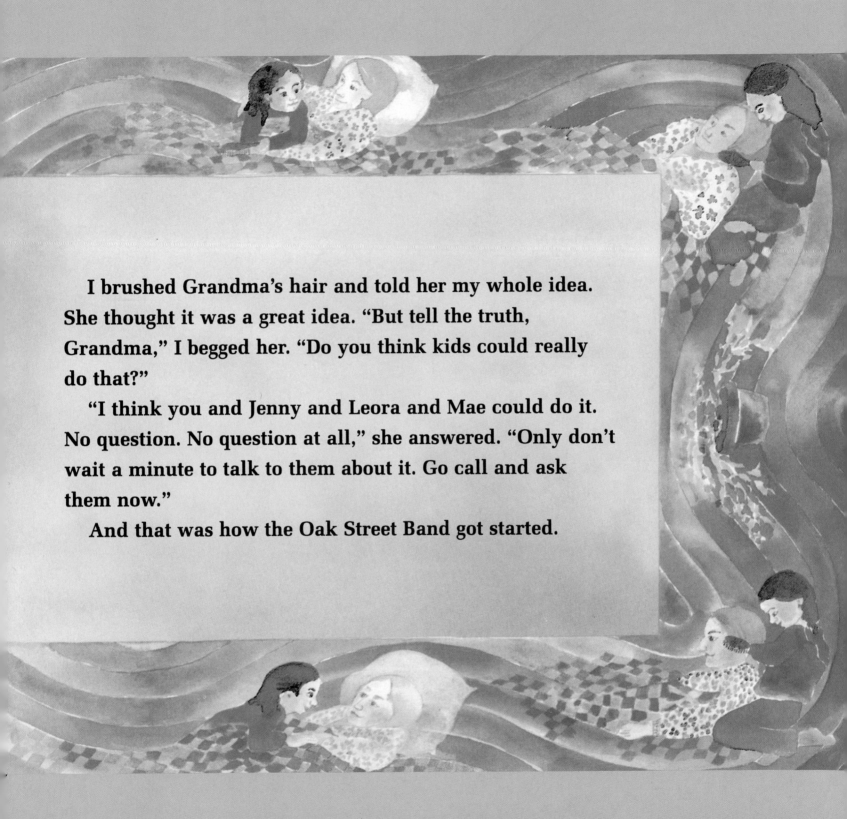

I brushed Grandma's hair and told her my whole idea. She thought it was a great idea. "But tell the truth, Grandma," I begged her. "Do you think kids could really do that?"

"I think you and Jenny and Leora and Mae could do it. No question. No question at all," she answered. "Only don't wait a minute to talk to them about it. Go call and ask them now."

And that was how the Oak Street Band got started.

Our music teachers helped us pick out pieces we could all play together. Aunt Ida, who plays guitar, helped us practice. We practiced on our back porch. One day our neighbor leaned out his window in his pajamas and yelled, "Listen, kids, you sound great but give me a break. I work at night. I've got to get some sleep in the daytime." After that we practiced inside. Grandma said it was helping her get better faster than anything.

At last my accordion teacher said we sounded very good. Uncle Sandy said so too. Aunt Ida and Grandma said we were terrific. Mama said she thought anyone would be glad to have us play for them.

It was Leora's mother who gave us our first job. She asked us to come and play at a party for Leora's great-grandmother and great-grandfather. It was going to be a special anniversary for them. It was fifty years ago on that day they first opened their market on our corner. Now Leora's mother takes care of the market. She always plays the radio loud while she works. But for the party she said there just had to be live music.

All of Leora's aunts and uncles and cousins came to the party. Lots of people from our block came too. Mama and Aunt Ida and Uncle Sandy walked down from our house very slowly with Grandma. It was Grandma's first big day out.

There was a long table in the backyard made from little tables all pushed together. It was covered with so many big dishes of food you could hardly see the tablecloth. But I was too excited to eat anything.

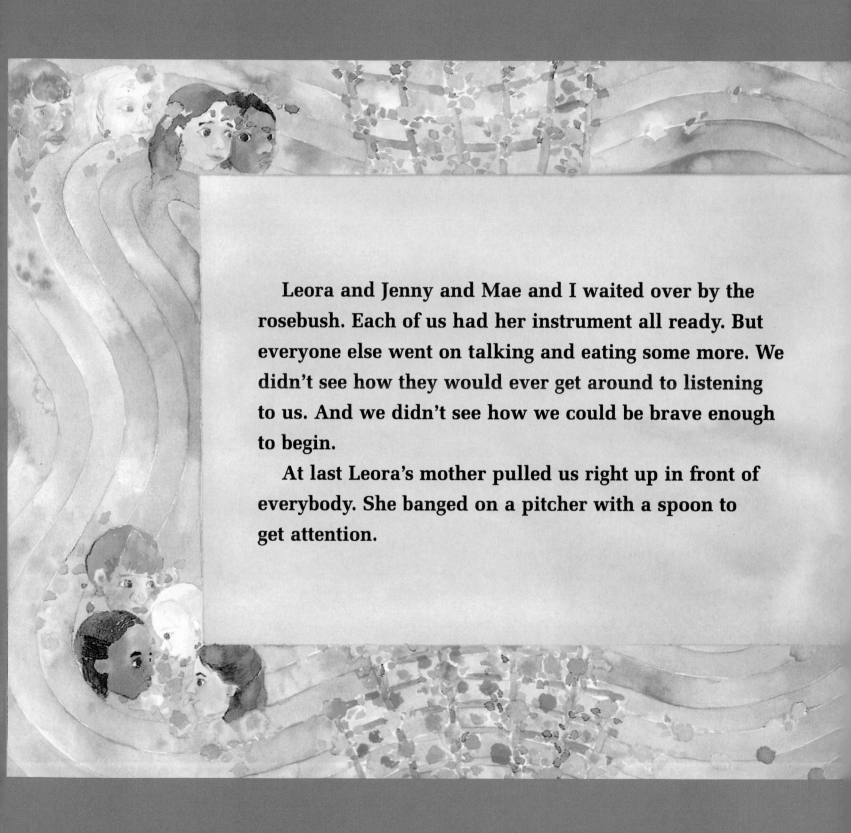

Leora and Jenny and Mae and I waited over by the rosebush. Each of us had her instrument all ready. But everyone else went on talking and eating some more. We didn't see how they would ever get around to listening to us. And we didn't see how we could be brave enough to begin.

At last Leora's mother pulled us right up in front of everybody. She banged on a pitcher with a spoon to get attention.

Then she introduced each one of us. "And *now* we're going to have music," she said. "Music and dancing for everyone."

It was quiet as school assembly. Every single person there was looking right at Leora and Jenny and Mae and me. But we just stood there and stared right back. Then I heard my grandma whisper, "Play, Pussycat. Play anything. Just like you used to play for me."

I put my fingers on the keys and buttons of my accordion. Jenny tucked her fiddle under her chin. Mae put her flute to her mouth. Leora held up her drums. After that we played and played. We made mistakes, but we played like a real band. The little lanterns came on. Everyone danced.

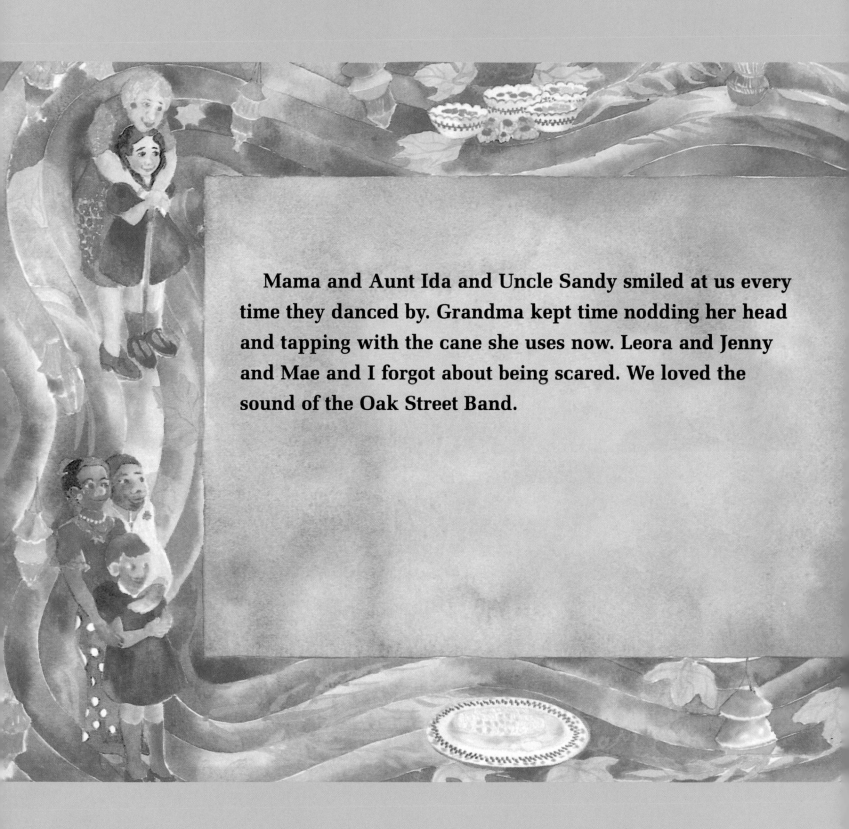

Mama and Aunt Ida and Uncle Sandy smiled at us every time they danced by. Grandma kept time nodding her head and tapping with the cane she uses now. Leora and Jenny and Mae and I forgot about being scared. We loved the sound of the Oak Street Band.

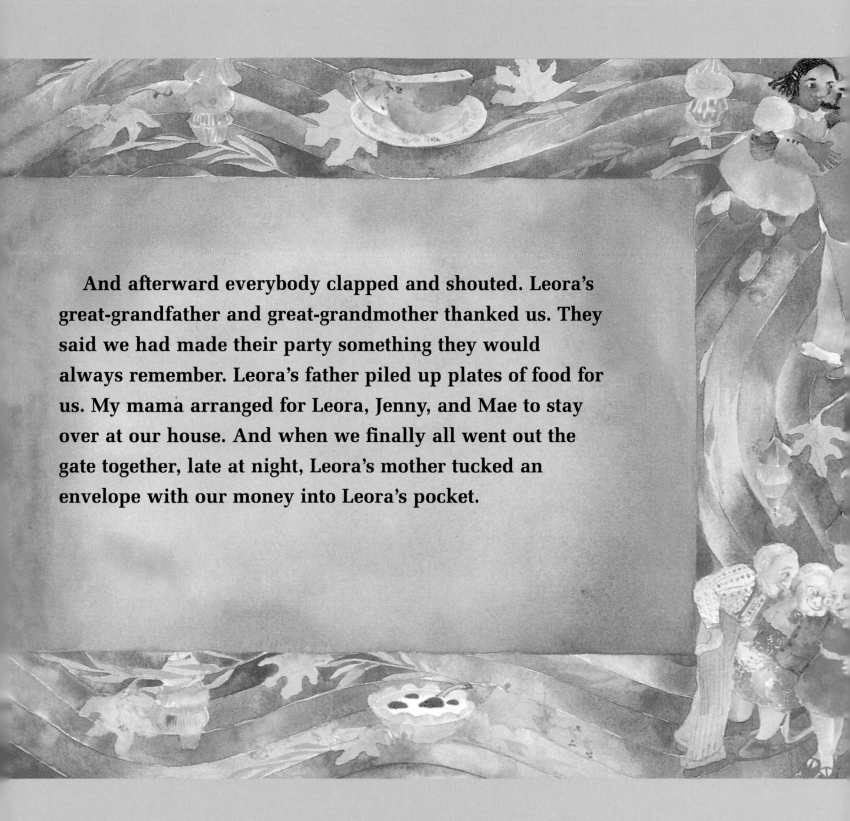

And afterward everybody clapped and shouted. Leora's great-grandfather and great-grandmother thanked us. They said we had made their party something they would always remember. Leora's father piled up plates of food for us. My mama arranged for Leora, Jenny, and Mae to stay over at our house. And when we finally all went out the gate together, late at night, Leora's mother tucked an envelope with our money into Leora's pocket.

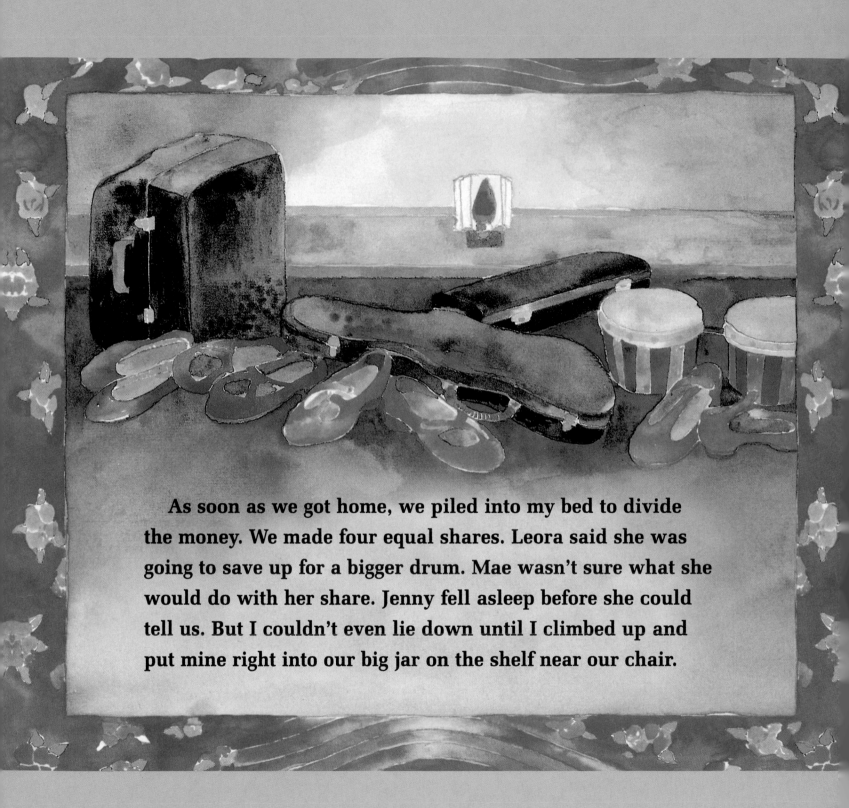

As soon as we got home, we piled into my bed to divide the money. We made four equal shares. Leora said she was going to save up for a bigger drum. Mae wasn't sure what she would do with her share. Jenny fell asleep before she could tell us. But I couldn't even lie down until I climbed up and put mine right into our big jar on the shelf near our chair.

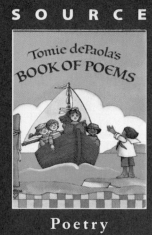

SOURCE

Tomie dePaola's
BOOK OF POEMS

Poetry
Collection

from **Tomie dePaola's**
Book of Poems

Celebration

by Alonzo Lopez
illustrated by Tomie dePaola

I shall dance tonight.
When the dusk comcs crawling.
There will be dancing
   and feasting.
I shall dance with the others
   in circles,
      in leaps,
         in stomps.
Laughter and talk
   will weave into the night,
Among the fires
   of my people.
Games will be played
And I shall be
   a part of it.

65

Cast and Crew

Performances combine the talents of many people.

Be amazed at all the different acts in one circus. Then look at a poster about a very different circus.

Follow three pigs step by step in the making of a puppet show.

Meet the woman who brings out the best in people on the stage and behind it.

CIRCUS GIRL   MICHAEL GARLAND

Alice is a circus girl. Everyone in her family is in the circus. Alice's mother walks the tightrope, and her father is a clown.

Alice and her mother and father live in a trailer.
They ride from town to town.
The circus travels around in a caravan filled
with people, animals, and all the equipment,
including the big tent—packed up for the ride.

When the circus comes to a new town, the elephants are paraded through the streets. Circus people put up signs and give out handbills to let everyone know when the show will begin.

Before the show, there is so
much work to be done.
Circus men put up the tent.
The performers practice
their acts, and the animals are
washed and brushed.
All the circus people help,
including Alice.

75

The show people put on their
costumes, and the clowns
paint their faces. Alice can't
decide what she wants to
be when she grows up—a
tightrope walker or a clown.

With a roll of the drums, the band starts to play. The show is ready to begin! The ringmaster, Alice's grandfather, leads the elephants into the big tent, followed by clowns, fancy horses, jugglers, acrobats, and all the others, in a grand procession around the three rings.

78

The townspeople cheer!
The children shout!

80

Then suddenly, the music stops. The ringmaster leaps into the center ring. "Ladies and gentlemen, and children of all ages…" he says in a loud voice, announcing the acts—something different in each ring.

83

Everyone loves the Famous Dancing Bears.
The biggest bear can even ride a motorcycle!

The Flying Gazpacho Brothers are Alice's uncles.
Their skill and balance astound the audience!

Alice holds the hoop for her Auntie Anne's Amazing
Performing Trick Dogs. Alice is so excited!

The lion tamer is very brave. When he cracks his whip, all the lions and tigers sit up and roll over.

The last and greatest act of all are the elephants. They entertain the audience with many clever feats. And then they lead the closing parade around the three rings. Other circus performers join them and wave good-bye. The townspeople cheer! The children shout! And then they go home.

The rings are swept clean, and the animals are back
in their pens and cages. The work is done.
The hungry circus people sit down to eat the dinner
that Alice's grandmother has cooked for them.

Everyone is tired, especially Alice. Her father reads
her a bedtime story before she goes to sleep. Alice
has to get up early in the morning because the
circus is going to another town—maybe yours!

Posters let us know that the circus is coming soon.

Art: Robdt Wallis · Nappi/Hanan Abstractung

Lincoln Center

OCT 20 – JAN 8

BIG APPLE CIRCUS IS A NOT-FOR-PROFIT PERFORMING ARTS ORGANIZATION

The Little Pigs' PUPPET BOOK

by N. Cameron Watson

It is raining. The three brothers stare out the window.

"Bother!" says Charles.

"What a gloomy day," grunts Ralph.

"We could always read," remarks Bertram.

"I have a better idea," exclaims Charles. "Let's put on a puppet show!"

"First," says Bertram, "we have to make some puppets."
Each pig has a plan. Charles uses a sock for his puppet.
Bertram starts with a cardboard tube. Ralph decides on a
jaw puppet.

When the puppets are finished, the pigs confer on
story ideas. Charles wants to make up a story as they
go along. Bertram would prefer using a fairy tale.

The brothers finally agree on an original plot.
Ralph writes a script on his computer.

The pigs begin to rehearse. Ralph gets grumpy
when Charles can't remember his lines. Charles
thinks Ralph is too bossy. But Bertram keeps them
going, and finally the play comes together nicely.

"How about building a stage?" says Ralph. Charles wants to set up a quick stage behind the table. Ralph suggests using a box. Bertram insists on making a stage to fit in the doorway. They all get to work.

The stage looks beautiful. "Bertram was right," admits Ralph.

"A stage like that needs some proper scenery," says
Charles. He gathers his materials and begins.

"Then we'll need music, programs, tickets, and, of
course, some refreshments," pronounces Bertram.
He makes up the programs and tickets while Charles
retires backstage to set everything up. Ralph goes to
the kitchen to prepare some special treats.

The show begins. Charles is nervous, but then he
speaks his first line, and the performance is off to a
promising start. The audience is enthralled.

After the show, everyone stays for refreshments.
Charles's wonderful puppet is passed around. Bertram's
fine design and lettering on the programs are admired.

Several older pigs approach Ralph and give the
budding young author their congratulations. The
evening has been a great success.

Outside it is dark, and the sky is clearing.
Tomorrow will be a fine, sunny day. But the
brothers are eagerly awaiting the next rainy day
and what it might bring.

Special Effects

Lighting

Make room dark. Light only the stage opening, so attention will be focused there. Set up one light on each side of stage front. Make sure they do not block view of stage. Use:

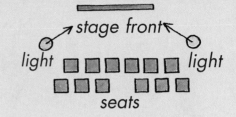

 clamp-on spotlights

floor lamps

a flashlight (held by a friend)

Bulb Color	Mood/Effect
white	normal/daylight
yellow	warm/coziness
blue	cold/moonlight
red	hot/scariness

Music

Use music to set the mood of the play and of each scene.

 piano

 recorder

 drum

 homemade rattle (coins in a jar)

 tape recorder

Sound Effects

Use your imagination! Here are some ideas:

thunder: drum; rattle a cookie sheet

crash: clang pots and utensils together

engine: coffee grinder or blender

thud: slap hand on floor

wind: blow over a bottle

footsteps: tap fingers on floor

Props

Make props from materials around the house, or use real objects. For example:

car: cardboard mounted on a flat stick, held from below

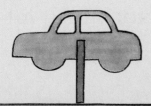

soda can: cardboard tube with added bottom and top

paintbrush: use a real one

flower: tissue paper, wooden skewer, and wire

103

Judith Martin

Theater Director

Curtain up!
On with the show!

Would you wear a costume made from paper bags? The Paper Bag Players do! They are a theater company that creates plays for children. They really do make their costumes from paper and cardboard.

Before children come to see a play, Judith Martin, the director, has a lot of work to do.

104

Questions

Here's how director Judith Martin works with her team to put on plays.

Q How do you get your ideas for plays?

A I try to think about what would make children laugh and what they would really like to see. Sometimes I go to schools and do theater with the children. They have many ideas about what makes a good play.

Q What happens after you decide on an idea?

A I write the script with all the lines that the actors will say. They practice their lines while I watch.

106

Q **Who else works on the play?**

A While the actors are practicing, our artist makes the props—all from paper or cardboard. I also tell her what kinds of costumes the actors need. Our musician writes and plays the music for the show and teaches it to the actors.

Q **What's the day of the first performance like?**

A The actors look great in their costumes. They know their lines and the music. And now it's the audience's turn to be part of the team. At some point in the play, the children are invited to join in somehow—maybe to dance!

Judith Martin's Tips for Young Directors

1 Work with your group to find a good story or write one about something funny that really happened.

2 Use homemade or old clothes for costumes.

3 Clear part of a room for a stage, and set up chairs for your audience.

Showtime!

Clear plans and directions help team members create projects.

Find out how much hard work goes into any movie that you see!

Choose a character you want to be in this read-aloud play. Then see where the ideas for the costumes came from.

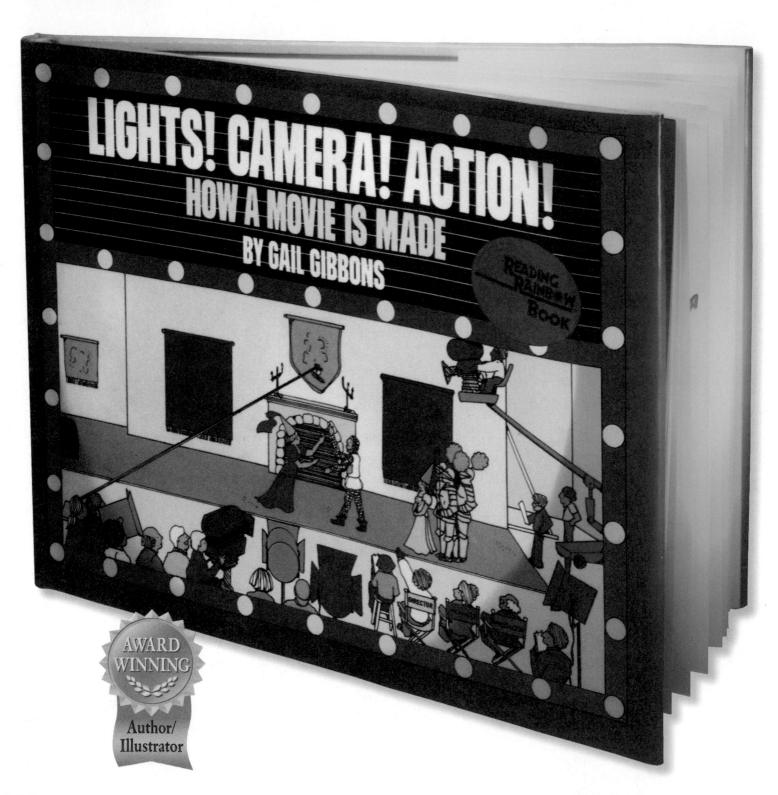

LIGHTS! CAMERA! ACTION!
HOW A MOVIE IS MADE
BY GAIL GIBBONS

READING RAINBOW BOOK

AWARD WINNING
Author/ Illustrator

The story is perfect! It is exactly what the
movie producers have been looking for. They
want to take the story and make it into a movie.

The producers hire the people they will need to
get started.

It could take millions of dollars to make the movie. The producers describe their project to people who might lend them money. That's how they get their "financial backing."

A major movie studio also likes the project. They will back the movie, too. And when the movie is finished, they will rent out copies to movie theaters.

Step 1: Pre-production...

Now the work begins. The producers hire a scriptwriter. It takes a long time to turn a story into a script, or screenplay. All the dialogue for the actresses and actors is written in the script along with technical directions for lighting, camera angles, and scene changes.

Next, the casting director is hired. She finds actors and actresses to play the leading parts. Sometimes the people chosen are very famous...stars!

There are tryouts for the smaller parts.

The producers need to find just the right locations
for the different scenes. Then the production manager
makes a schedule for filming them.

Sketches are made.

The pre-production crew is bigger now.
The different departments work to get everything
ready. The costume designers, the lighting technicians,

the property department, the set designers,

the sound technicians, and the special effects
department rush to meet the production deadline.

The actresses and actors rehearse...

and rehearse their lines.

Finally, after months of work, everyone and everything is ready. It is time for the different scenes to be filmed.

They will not be shot in the order of the script. All the scenes in the same location, or on the same set, will be shot together. It is easier and costs less that way. When the filming is over, the scenes will be put together in order again.

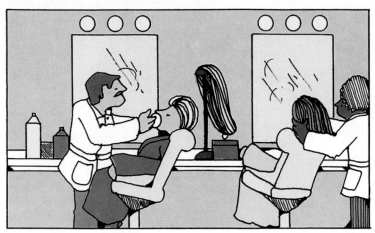

The actresses and actors arrive early each morning.
In the dressing rooms, makeup artists and hair
stylists get them ready for the day's shooting.
Wardrobe assistants help them into their costumes.

Meanwhile, over on the set, the camera operators are in position. The sound technicians are adjusting their equipment. The lighting technicians, called gaffers, have set up the lights.

The actors and actresses come in.

The scene is rehearsed one last time.

Step 2: Production...

Everything looks right.

The director gives a signal. The assistant director yells, "Quiet on the set!"

Production begins.
Lights! Camera! Action!

The director yells, "Cut!" Somebody missed
a line.
 They reshoot the scene until it is perfect.
 "Print it!" the director yells. He likes the take.

At the end of the day, all the takes are rushed to the film processing lab to be printed.

Each day's film is called a daily. Every morning the producers and director view the dailies from the day before.

Step 3: Post-production...

Once all the scenes have been shot, the film editors take over. They go through the reels and reels of film and select what they need. If it isn't just right, it is out.

The edited film is spliced together in the order of the scenes in the script.

The producers and director view the film. They all agree—it's just what they want. It works!

Dubbing console

Next, music must be added to the sound track.
A composer is hired. The music he creates will set
the mood for the film.

Any mistakes in the dialogue can be corrected now.

Mixers put the music, dialogue, and sound effects
together.

Then the complete sound track will be added to
the film.

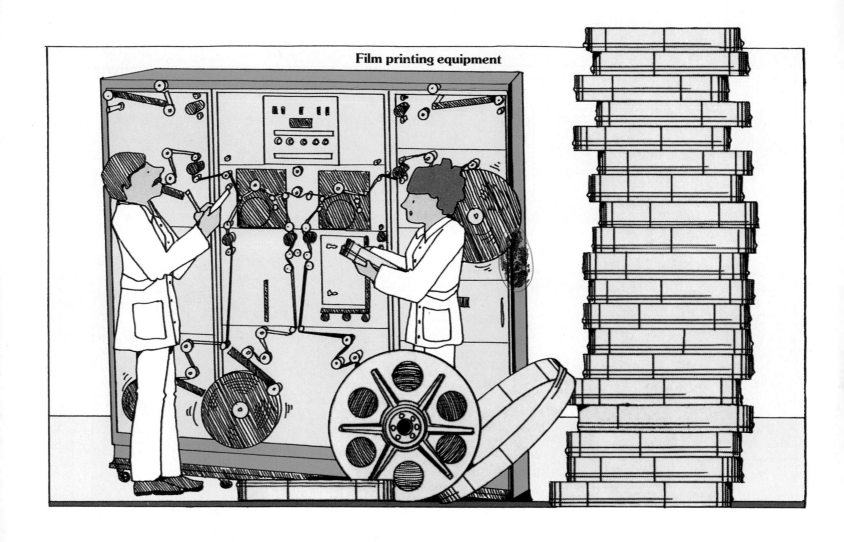

Film printing equipment

The movie is completed.

The first print, called an answer print, is made and given one final check. Then thousands of copies, called release prints, are made.

The movie studio will rent out these copies to the
movie theaters. For months, the studio has been
advertising the movie and stirring up interest with
a big publicity campaign.

The premier showing is held at a big city theater. The stars are there. All the people who made the movie are there, too.

Fans and movie critics come to the glamorous event.

The audience waits.

The lights go out and the movie begins.

THE SWALLOW'S ▶ GIFT ◀

A Play from a Korean Folk Tale
By Lindy Soon Curry
Illustrated by Yumi Heo

AWARD
WINNING

Illustrator

CHARACTERS

Narrator
Nolbu, selfish older brother
Hungbu, kind younger brother
Mother, wife of Hungbu
Sister, daughter of Hungbu
Brother, son of Hungbu
Swallow

NARRATOR

Long ago in old Korea, two brothers lived together in a large house that their father had built. For many years they got along well. Then one winter day Nolbu got angry and ordered his younger brother Hungbu to move out.

Our play begins as Hungbu and his family set out in search of a new place to live.

SISTER
We have been walking for such a long time.

BROTHER
I'm so cold and tired. Where will we sleep tonight?

HUNGBU
Don't worry children. Here is a shack. You gather leaves and branches. Mother and I will patch the cracks and make the house cozy and warm.

MOTHER
By working together, we'll make it through the winter. But each of us must help.

SISTER
I'll help clean the house.

BROTHER
I'll gather firewood.

NARRATOR

After a long cold winter, Hungbu and his family were glad to see spring arrive. They planted a garden and watched a pair of swallows build a nest on their roof. One day while they were gardening . . .

BROTHER

Look! This baby swallow fell out of the nest in our roof. I think its leg is broken.

HUNGBU

Baby swallow, don't be afraid. I'll help you. Let me bandage your leg with this cloth.

(He takes a piece of cloth and wraps it around the bird's leg.)

SWALLOW
Thank you. That feels much better.

BROTHER
Here's a bowl of water. Please drink some and get well quickly.

SISTER
Little swallow, eat some sesame seeds. They will make you strong.

SWALLOW
Ah! I feel better already.

MOTHER
You may sleep in this basket until you are strong enough to fly again.

SWALLOW
I'll always remember your kindness.

143

NARRATOR

The swallow was soon well enough to fly away. But one year later, the little bird returned to thank Hungbu and his family.

BROTHER

Father! There's the swallow with the crooked leg. It's hopping up to you.

HUNGBU

It has a pumpkin seed in its beak.

(He takes the seed from the bird.)

Thank you, swallow.

SWALLOW

This is a gift to thank you for taking care of me.

MOTHER

We'll plant it right away. I'll dig the hole.

SISTER

I'll cover the seed with dirt.

BROTHER

I'll water it and see that it is weeded.

NARRATOR

That night as the family slept, the swallow's seed
sprouted, and it grew and grew. In the morning,
Hungbu and his family awoke to an amazing sight.

MOTHER

Look outside! There's a big green plant . . .

SISTER

. . . with three yellow blossoms . . .

BROTHER

. . . that are turning into yellow pumpkins!

(Hungbu goes away and returns with a long saw.)

HUNGBU

Children, if you will help Mother and me,
we can saw through this big pumpkin.

NARRATOR

And so they pushed and pulled and pushed
and pulled until the first pumpkin fell open.

MOTHER
I see something glittering inside!

HUNGBU
Gold!

SISTER
Rubies!

BROTHER
Emeralds!

MOTHER
Let's open the
second pumpkin.

NARRATOR
They pushed and pulled on the saw.

BROTHER
I hear something rattling!

NARRATOR
And the second pumpkin fell open.

HUNGBU
Rice! Thousands of grains of rice!

MOTHER
Now we can eat, eat, eat!

BROTHER
Until our bellies are full, full, full!

SISTER
Let's open the third pumpkin.

NARRATOR
Once again, they pushed and pulled until the third and last pumpkin fell open.

MOTHER
Oooh! Yards and yards of silk! Let's make beautiful clothes and stroll into town.

NARRATOR
News traveled fast. When Nolbu heard about his brother's good fortune, he went to visit Hungbu.

NOLBU
How did you get all these riches?

HUNGBU
We took care of a swallow with a broken leg. It rewarded us with a seed that grew pumpkins filled with wonderful things. Come live with us, brother. There is plenty for everyone.

NOLBU
No. I'll find my own fortune.

NARRATOR
And Nolbu stormed off to search for a swallow.

NOLBU
Here's a swallow with a crooked leg.

(Nolbu quickly and roughly ties a cloth around the bird's leg.)

NOLBU
Now fly away and bring me back a seed. Make me richer than my brother.

SWALLOW
Ouch, you hurt me! I'll always remember this.

NARRATOR
The following spring, the bird returned to Nolbu and brought him a seed.

SWALLOW
Here's your reward as you wished.

NOLBU
I'll be rich, rich, rich!

NARRATOR

Nolbu planted his seed and it grew just as fast as Hungbu's did, but only two pumpkins sprouted from it instead of three. Nolbu had trouble cutting the pumpkins open because he was all alone. He had no one to help him.

(The first pumpkin breaks open.)

NOLBU

This pumpkin is rotten! It smells terrible! I must open the second one. Perhaps that one will be full of money.

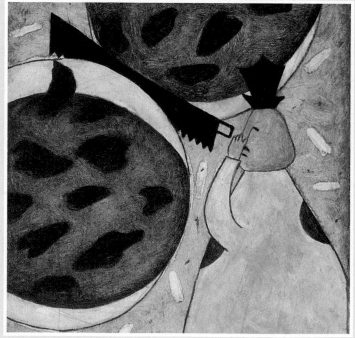

(Nolbu saws the second pumpkin until it falls open.)

NOLBU
Yuck! Spiders and snakes and scorpions!
They are crawling over everything!
I can't live in this house anymore.
Maybe Hungbu will let me live with
him after all.

NARRATOR
Nolbu returned to his brother's house
and knocked on the door.

HUNGBU

Welcome, brother! Please come in.

NOLBU

I am sorry for the way I treated you.
Now my house is full of bugs and
snakes. May I live with you?

HUNGBU

Yes, please join us. I'm sorry for what
has happened to you.

NOLBU

I'll always work and share equally
with you.

HUNGBU

That's the way our father wanted us
to live.

NARRATOR

From that day on, the two brothers
lived together under the same roof
happily ever after.

A Long Ago Look

SOURCE

Korean
Reference Book

Here's clothing that Korean men and women wore a long, long time ago. Koreans often wore light-colored pieces of clothing. What they wore depended upon how much money they had. Today in Korea, clothing like this from long ago is worn by older people on special holidays.

Glossary

accordion
a musical instrument with a keyboard played with one hand and a bellows pushed in and out with the other hand

She played a lively tune on her new **accordion**.

acrobats
performers who do exciting tricks, such as walking on a wire high above the ground

The **acrobats** fly through the air.

acrobats

actors
people who perform in plays, movies, or TV stories

The **actors** in this movie are very good.

actresses
women or girls who perform in plays, movies, or TV stories

We need three more **actresses** for our school play.

assistants
helpers

The doctor had two **assistants** who helped her take care of sick people.

clowns
performers who dress in funny clothes and do tricks to make people laugh

The **clowns** wore silly hats and shoes and big red noses.

clowns

composer
a person who makes up music

The **composer** sat at the piano to play his new song.

cowards
people who are afraid of anything that is dangerous or hard to do

They felt like **cowards** for not climbing all the way to the top.

danger
something that could hurt you

The rabbit crossing the busy road is in **danger**.

director
the person who tells the actors what to do in a movie or play

The **director** told the actor to speak louder.

dreadful
scary, terrible

The angry tiger was a **dreadful** thing to see.

drums
musical instruments played by beating with sticks

The musician moved his sticks quickly across his **drums.**

emeralds

emeralds
bright green jewels or the stones they are made from

Emeralds are worth a lot of money.

fiddle
a musical instrument played by moving a bow across the strings

He picked up the bow to play his **fiddle**.

fierce
wild and dangerous

Angry animals are sometimes **fierce**.

flute
a long, thin musical instrument played by blowing through one end and placing fingers over the holes

Her fingers were moving slowly as she played the **flute**.

flutes

fortune
a lot of money

The rich man gave some of his **fortune** to help poor people.

gruesome
scary and horrible

The monster's face was **gruesome**.

guitar
a musical instrument played by moving the fingers across the strings

The performer played the **guitar** and sang.

instrument
something used to make music

The piano is my favorite **instrument**.

jugglers

jugglers
performers who do tricks with things they throw and catch

The **jugglers** could keep four pins up in the air at one time.

kindness
being nice and helpful to others

The old woman was loved by all for her **kindness**.

performers
people who do something to entertain others

The jugglers, acrobats, and clowns are all **performers** in the circus.

producers
people who get a movie, show, or play ready to be seen

Producers hire the actors, writers, and directors for movies.

guitar

programs
small booklets that tell about a show

The **programs** tell who is in the play and what they will do.

rehearse
to practice a play or other show before presenting it to an audience

We had to **rehearse** our play many times.

rewarded
having received money or treats for good work or kind acts

The boy who saved the puppy was **rewarded** with ten dollars.

riches
money and things that are worth a lot of money

The king had jewels and other **riches**.

ringmaster
the person at the circus who tells about the performers

The **ringmaster** told us about the jugglers.

rubies
bright red jewels

The **rubies** in her necklace were beautiful.

scared
afraid, frightened

The cat was **scared** of falling in the water.

scenery
painted walls, hangings, or other things that are put on a stage to show where the play takes place

The **scenery** for the play showed the inside of the king's castle.

script
a written copy of what actors say in a play, movie, or TV or radio show

The actors had to read the **script** until they learned what to say.

stage
the place where actors, dancers, or singers perform

The singers and dancers were all on the **stage** at once.

technicians
people who can use or fix machines

The people who take care of the sound at a music show are **technicians**.

terror
strong fear

The hunter felt **terror** when the bear ran after him.

Authors and Illustrators

Gail Gibbons pages 110–137

Gail Gibbons used to work at a TV station. She had a lot of fun creating art for a children's show. This made her decide to write and illustrate a children's book. Now she works all the time on children's books about many different subjects. Books by Gibbons include *Weather Words and What They Mean* and *Beacons of Light: Lighthouses.*

Yumi Heo pages 138–152

Yumi Heo says that *The Swallow's Gift* is a tale she has known and loved since she was a little girl in Korea. Heo also remembers getting her first box of crayons. She was five then, and she has been creating colorful pictures ever since. Another tale with pictures by Heo is *The Rabbit's Judgment* by Suzanne Crowder Han.

Hans Wilhelm pages 10-35

Hans Wilhelm grew up in Bremen, Germany—the very same town in which *The Bremen Town Musicians* takes place! He says that he likes writing funny stories and drawing pictures to match. His book *Tyrone the Horrible* is about a dinosaur that is a bully. In *Bad, Bad Bunny Trouble*, a bunny who loves soccer plays a trick on three hungry foxes.

Vera B. Williams pages 36-64

Vera B. Williams wrote and illustrated her first book in high school. It was about a giant banana! Most of this author's books are about things that happened to her. She says that the character of Rosa reminds her of herself as a little girl. Two other books about Rosa and her family are *A Chair for My Mother* and *Something Special for Me*.

159

Acknowledgments

Grateful acknowledgment is made to the following sources for permission to reprint from previously published material. The publisher has made diligent efforts to trace the ownership of all copyrighted material in this volume and believes that all necessary permissions have been secured. If any errors or omissions have inadvertently been made, proper corrections will gladly be made in future editions.

Cover: Photo: © Tracey Wheeler for Scholastic Inc. Border illustration: Anthony De Angelos.

Interior: The "Bremen Town Musicians" from THE BREMEN TOWN MUSICIANS by Hans Wilhelm. Copyright © 1992 by Hans Wilhelm, Inc. Reprinted by permission of Scholastic Inc.

"Music, Music For Everyone" from MUSIC, MUSIC FOR EVERYONE by Vera B. Williams. Copyright © 1984 by Vera B. Williams. By permission of Greenwillow Books, a division of William Morrow & Company, Inc.

"Celebration" by Alonzo Lopez from WHISPERING WIND by Terry Allen. Text copyright © 1972 by the Institute of American Indian Arts. Used by permission of Doubleday, a division of Bantam Doubleday Dell Publishing Group, Inc. Cover and illustrations by Tomie dePaola from TOMIE DEPAOLA'S BOOK OF POEMS. Illustrations copyright © 1988 by Tomie dePaola. Reprinted by permission of G. P. Putnam's Sons.

"Circus Girl" from CIRCUS GIRL by Michael Garland. Copyright © 1993 by Michael Garland. Used by permission of Dutton Children's Books, a division of Penguin Books USA Inc.

Selections and cover from THE LITTLE PIGS' PUPPET BOOK by N. Cameron Watson. Copyright © 1990 by N. Cameron Watson. Reprinted by permission of Little, Brown and Company.

"Lights! Camera! Action! How a Movie is Made" from LIGHTS! CAMERA! ACTION! HOW A MOVIE IS MADE by Gail Gibbons. Copyright © 1985 by Gail Gibbons. Reprinted by permission of HarperCollins Publishers.

THE SWALLOW'S GIFT by Lindy Soon Curry, illustrated by Yumi Heo. Copyright © 1996 by Scholastic Inc.

Cover from BASEBALL BALLERINA by Kathryn Cristaldi, illustrated by Abby Carter. Illustration copyright © 1992 by Abby Carter. Published by Random House, Inc.

Cover from THE BUNNY PLAY by Loreen Leedy. Illustration copyright © 1988 by Loreen Leedy. Published by Holiday House, Inc.

Cover from SHEEP DREAMS by Arthur A. Levine, illustrated by Judy Lanfredi. Illustration copyright © 1993 by Judy Lanfredi. Published by Dial Books for Young Readers, a division of Penguin Books USA Inc.

Cover from SONG AND DANCE MAN by Karen Ackerman, illustrated by Stephen Gammell. Illustration copyright © 1988 by Stephen Gammell. Published by Alfred A. Knopf, Inc.

Photography and Illustration Credits

Selection Opener Photographs by David S. Waitz Photography/Alleycat Design, Inc.

Photos: p. 3 br: © Andrew M. Levine for Scholastic Inc. pp.2-3: © Scott Heiser/Courtesy, The Paper Bag Players. pp.8-9: © Stanley Bach for Scholastic Inc. pp.8-9 background: © Christian Michaels/FPG International Corp. pp.66-67 c: © Stanley Bach for Scholastic Inc. pp.92-92 c: Courtesy of Big Apple Circus. p. 104 bl: © Martha Swope for Scholastic Inc.; tl: © Scott Heiser/Courtesy, The Paper Bag Players. pp.104-105 tc: © Andrew M. Levine for Scholastic Inc. p. 105 br: Andrew M. Levine for Scholastic Inc.p. 106 cl: Martha Swope for Scholastic Inc. pp. 106-107 bc: Martha Swope for Scholastic Inc. p. 107 tr,cr: © Andrew M. Levine for Scholastic Inc.; br: © Martha Swope for Scholastic Inc. pp. 108-109: © Stanley Bach for Scholastic Inc. p. 153 cr, cl, tr: Courtesy of Yegyong Sanopsa/Pascal Andre for Scholastic Inc. p. 154 tc: © Haroldo de Faria/FPG International Corp.; br: © M. Keller/The Stock Market. p. 155 c: © Carl Frank, 1972/Photo Researchers, Inc.; br: © Kathy Sloane/Photo Researchers, Inc. p. 156 tc: © Michael Newman/PhotoEdit; bl: © David S. Waitz for Scholastic Inc. p. 158 bl: © Courtesy of Holiday House; p. 158 br: © Courtesy of Yumi Heo; p. 159 Hans Wilhelm: Courtesy of Scholastic Trade Department; br; © Courtesy of William Morrow & Company.

Illustrations: pp. 2-3: Jackie Snider; p. 92: Brian Dugan.